EMMANUEL JOSEPH

The Nexus of Power, Uniting Political Theory, Social Dynamics, and Corporate Vision

First edition

This book was professionally typeset on Reedsy.
Find out more at reedsy.com

Contents

1

Chapter 1: The Foundation of Power

Power, in its various forms, has shaped the human experience from the dawn of civilization. This chapter explores the essence of power, examining the multifaceted nature that permeates political, social, and economic structures. We delve into historical perspectives, drawing on ancient philosophies and modern theories that seek to define and contextualize power. Understanding the foundational elements of power allows us to appreciate the intricate dance between individuals, societies, and institutions.

As we journey through the historical landscape, we uncover the enduring influence of seminal thinkers such as Machiavelli, Hobbes, and Marx. Their perspectives offer invaluable insights into the mechanisms of power and control. The chapter also introduces key concepts like authority, legitimacy, and sovereignty, which are central to our understanding of political power. By tracing the evolution of these ideas, we lay the groundwork for a deeper exploration of power in contemporary contexts.

Moreover, this chapter emphasizes the interplay between power and identity. It highlights how power dynamics are influenced by factors such as race, gender, and class, and how these intersections shape our social realities. The discussion extends to the impact of power on individual agency and collective action, illuminating the ways in which power can both liberate and oppress. Through a critical examination of these dynamics, we gain a nuanced understanding of the complexities of power.

In conclusion, the foundation of power is not a monolithic construct but a dynamic and evolving phenomenon. By examining its historical roots and contemporary manifestations, we set the stage for a comprehensive analysis of power's role in shaping our world. This foundational understanding is crucial as we navigate the intricate relationships between political theory, social dynamics, and corporate vision.

2

Chapter 2: Political Ideologies and Power Structures

Political ideologies shape our understanding of power and influence the structures that govern societies. This chapter delves into the core principles of major political ideologies, such as liberalism, conservatism, socialism, and anarchism. By examining their historical development and contemporary relevance, we gain insight into how these ideologies inform power dynamics.

We explore the role of political institutions in maintaining or challenging power structures. From democratic systems that promote participation and accountability to authoritarian regimes that centralize control, the chapter highlights the diverse ways in which power is exercised and legitimized. Through case studies and comparative analyses, we uncover the strengths and weaknesses of different political systems.

Furthermore, this chapter addresses the impact of political ideologies on policy-making and governance. It examines how ideologies shape the priorities and decisions of political leaders, influencing everything from economic policies to social welfare programs. By understanding these dynamics, we can better appreciate the complex interplay between political theory and practical governance.

In conclusion, political ideologies and power structures are integral to our understanding of how societies function. By critically examining these ideologies and their influence on political institutions, we gain a deeper appreciation of the diverse ways in which power can be organized and exercised.

3

Chapter 3: The Role of Social Movements

Social movements have the power to challenge existing power structures and drive transformative change. This chapter explores the origins, development, and impact of social movements, from historical examples like the civil rights movement to contemporary movements such as Black Lives Matter and climate activism.

We analyze the strategies and tactics employed by social movements to mobilize support and achieve their goals. From grassroots organizing to digital activism, the chapter highlights the diverse methods through which social movements can influence public opinion and policy. By examining the successes and challenges faced by these movements, we gain valuable insights into the dynamics of collective action.

Moreover, this chapter addresses the role of social movements in shaping societal values and norms. It explores how movements can challenge dominant narratives and promote alternative visions of justice, equality, and freedom. Through case studies and theoretical perspectives, we uncover the ways in which social movements can create lasting social change.

In conclusion, social movements are powerful agents of change that play a crucial role in shaping the social and political landscape. By understanding their origins, strategies, and impact, we can better appreciate the potential for collective action to challenge and transform power structures.

4

Chapter 4: Corporate Power and Capitalism

Corporate power is a defining feature of modern capitalism, shaping economies and societies in profound ways. This chapter examines the origins and development of corporate power, exploring how corporations have become central actors in the global economy.

We analyze the ways in which corporations exercise power, from their influence on policy-making to their impact on labor markets and environmental sustainability. The chapter highlights the mechanisms through which corporations can shape public opinion and drive economic growth, as well as the ethical and social challenges posed by corporate power.

Furthermore, this chapter addresses the role of corporate governance in shaping corporate behavior. It examines the principles and practices of corporate governance, exploring how different models of governance can influence corporate decision-making and accountability. Through case studies and theoretical perspectives, we gain insights into the dynamics of corporate power and its implications for society.

In conclusion, corporate power is a central feature of modern capitalism, with far-reaching implications for economies and societies. By critically examining the origins, exercise, and governance of corporate power, we can better understand its impact and explore strategies for promoting more equitable and sustainable forms of capitalism.

5

Chapter 5: The Interplay of Politics and Economics

The relationship between politics and economics is a complex and dynamic one, with profound implications for power and governance. This chapter explores the interplay between political and economic systems, examining how political decisions shape economic outcomes and vice versa.

We analyze the role of the state in regulating and shaping economic activity, from policies that promote economic growth to those that address inequality and social welfare. The chapter highlights the diverse ways in which governments can influence economic behavior, from taxation and regulation to public investment and social programs.

Furthermore, this chapter addresses the impact of economic globalization on political power. It examines the ways in which global economic integration can reshape the balance of power between states, corporations, and other actors. Through case studies and theoretical perspectives, we uncover the ways in which economic forces can both enhance and constrain political authority.

In conclusion, the interplay of politics and economics is a central feature of contemporary governance, with profound implications for power and policy-making. By understanding the dynamics of this relationship, we can better appreciate the challenges and opportunities it presents for promoting more inclusive and sustainable forms of development.

6

Chapter 6: Power in the Digital Age

The digital age has revolutionized the way power is exercised and distributed. This chapter explores the transformative impact of technology on power dynamics, from the rise of social media to the proliferation of big data and artificial intelligence. We examine how digital platforms can empower individuals and communities while also presenting new challenges for privacy, security, and control.

We analyze the role of tech giants in shaping the digital landscape, highlighting their influence on public opinion, economic activity, and political discourse. The chapter also addresses the ethical implications of technological advancements, exploring issues such as algorithmic bias, data privacy, and the digital divide. By examining these dynamics, we gain a deeper understanding of the complex interplay between technology and power.

Moreover, this chapter considers the potential for digital technologies to enhance democratic participation and accountability. It explores the ways in which technology can facilitate civic engagement, transparency, and collective action. Through case studies and theoretical perspectives, we uncover the potential for digital tools to reshape power structures and promote social change.

In conclusion, the digital age presents both opportunities and challenges for the exercise of power. By critically examining the impact of technology on power dynamics, we can better navigate the complex and rapidly evolving digital landscape.

7

Chapter 7: Globalization and Geopolitical Power

Globalization has reshaped the balance of power on the global stage, creating new opportunities and challenges for states, corporations, and other actors. This chapter examines the impact of globalization on geopolitical power, exploring how economic, political, and cultural forces intersect in a globalized world.

We analyze the ways in which globalization has transformed traditional power structures, from the rise of multinational corporations to the emergence of transnational networks and organizations. The chapter highlights the complexities of global governance, exploring the roles of international institutions, regional organizations, and non-state actors in shaping global power dynamics.

Furthermore, this chapter addresses the impact of globalization on inequality and social justice. It examines how global economic integration can exacerbate disparities between and within countries, while also creating new opportunities for cooperation and development. Through case studies and theoretical perspectives, we uncover the ways in which globalization can both empower and marginalize different actors.

In conclusion, globalization has profound implications for the exercise of power on the global stage. By understanding the dynamics of globalization and its impact on geopolitical power, we can better appreciate the opportunities and challenges it presents for promoting more inclusive and sustainable forms of development.

8

Chapter 8: The Influence of Media and Public Opinion

Media and public opinion play a crucial role in shaping power dynamics, influencing everything from political decisions to corporate behavior. This chapter explores the power of media in shaping public perception and opinion, examining how different forms of media—from traditional newspapers to social media platforms—can shape and reflect societal values.

We analyze the role of media in shaping political discourse, highlighting the ways in which media coverage can influence public opinion and policy-making. The chapter also addresses the ethical responsibilities of journalists and media organizations, exploring issues such as media bias, misinformation, and the role of the press in a democratic society.

Moreover, this chapter considers the impact of public opinion on power dynamics. It examines how public opinion can influence political and corporate decisions, from electoral outcomes to corporate social responsibility initiatives. Through case studies and theoretical perspectives, we uncover the ways in which media and public opinion can both reflect and shape power structures.

In conclusion, media and public opinion are powerful forces that shape the exercise of power in contemporary societies. By critically examining the influence of media and public opinion, we can better understand the dynamics of power and the potential for media to promote accountability and social change.

9

Chapter 9: Environmental Policy and Power

Environmental policy is a critical area where power dynamics play out, influencing everything from climate change mitigation to resource management. This chapter examines the role of power in shaping environmental policy, exploring the ways in which different actors—from governments to corporations to civil society—exercise influence over environmental decisions.

We analyze the complexities of environmental governance, highlighting the challenges and opportunities of coordinating action at local, national, and global levels. The chapter addresses the role of international agreements, such as the Paris Agreement, in shaping environmental policy and promoting collective action to address global challenges.

Furthermore, this chapter considers the impact of power dynamics on environmental justice. It examines how environmental policies can disproportionately affect marginalized communities and the importance of promoting equity and inclusion in environmental decision-making. Through case studies and theoretical perspectives, we uncover the ways in which environmental policy can both reflect and challenge existing power structures.

In conclusion, environmental policy is a critical area where power dynamics play out, with profound implications for sustainability and social justice. By understanding the role of power in shaping environmental policy, we can better navigate the complexities of environmental governance and promote more equitable and sustainable outcomes.

10

Chapter 10: The Power of Education and Knowledge

E ducation and knowledge are powerful tools that shape the future of societies. This chapter explores the role of education in empowering individuals and communities, examining how access to knowledge can transform lives and promote social mobility.

We analyze the impact of education on power dynamics, highlighting the ways in which educational institutions can both reinforce and challenge existing power structures. The chapter addresses issues such as educational inequality, the role of curriculum in shaping societal values, and the importance of critical thinking and civic education in fostering an informed and engaged citizenry.

Furthermore, this chapter considers the role of knowledge production and dissemination in shaping power. It examines the ways in which academic research, media, and other forms of knowledge can influence public opinion and policy-making. Through case studies and theoretical perspectives, we uncover the ways in which education and knowledge can be leveraged to promote social change.

In conclusion, education and knowledge are crucial components of power, with profound implications for individual and societal development. By understanding the dynamics of education and knowledge, we can better appreciate their potential to empower and transform.

11

Chapter 11: Health, Power, and Social Justice

Health is a critical area where power dynamics play out, influencing everything from access to healthcare to health outcomes. This chapter examines the role of power in shaping health and social justice, exploring the ways in which different actors—from governments to healthcare providers to civil society—exercise influence over health policy and practice.

We analyze the complexities of health governance, highlighting the challenges and opportunities of promoting equitable and inclusive health systems. The chapter addresses issues such as health disparities, the social determinants of health, and the role of health policy in addressing these challenges.

Furthermore, this chapter considers the impact of power dynamics on health justice. It examines how health policies can disproportionately affect marginalized communities and the importance of promoting equity and inclusion in health decision-making. Through case studies and theoretical perspectives, we uncover the ways in which health policy can both reflect and challenge existing power structures.

In conclusion, health is a critical area where power dynamics play out, with profound implications for social justice and equity. By understanding the role of power in shaping health policy and practice, we can better navigate the complexities of health governance and promote more equitable health outcomes.

12

Chapter 12: Cultural Power and Identity

Culture is a powerful force that shapes our identities and influences power dynamics. This chapter explores the role of cultural power in shaping societal values, norms, and identities, examining how culture can both reflect and challenge existing power structures.

We analyze the ways in which cultural power is exercised, from the influence of media and entertainment to the role of cultural institutions and practices. The chapter addresses issues such as cultural appropriation, representation, and the impact of cultural power on marginalized communities.

Furthermore, this chapter considers the role of identity in shaping power dynamics. It examines how factors such as race, gender, sexuality, and nationality intersect to shape our experiences of power and oppression. Through case studies and theoretical perspectives, we uncover the ways in which cultural power and identity can both empower and marginalize different actors.

In conclusion, cultural power and identity are crucial components of power dynamics, with profound implications for individual and societal development. By understanding the dynamics of cultural power and identity, we can better appreciate their potential to empower and transform.

13

Chapter 13: Power Dynamics in the Workplace

The workplace is a key arena where power dynamics play out, influencing everything from employee relations to organizational performance. This chapter examines the role of power in shaping workplace dynamics, exploring the ways in which different actors—from employers to employees to unions—exercise influence over workplace decisions.

We analyze the complexities of workplace power, highlighting the challenges and opportunities of promoting equitable and inclusive work environments. The chapter addresses issues such as workplace hierarchies, the role of leadership, and the impact of power dynamics on employee well-being and productivity.

Furthermore, this chapter considers the role of labor rights and advocacy in shaping workplace power. It examines how labor movements and policies can influence workplace conditions and promote greater equity and inclusion. Through case studies and theoretical perspectives, we uncover the ways in which workplace power can both reflect and challenge existing power structures.

In conclusion, power dynamics in the workplace are a critical area where power is exercised, with profound implications for organizational and individual development. By understanding the role of power in shaping workplace dynamics, we can better navigate the complexities of work environments and promote more equitable and inclusive workplaces.

14

Chapter 14: Gender and Power

Gender plays a crucial role in shaping power dynamics, influencing everything from political representation to workplace hierarchies. This chapter examines the intersection of gender and power, exploring how gendered norms and stereotypes shape our experiences of power and oppression.

We analyze the ways in which gender influences access to power, highlighting the challenges and opportunities for promoting gender equality. The chapter addresses issues such as gender-based violence, the gender pay gap, and the role of gender in shaping political and corporate leadership.

Furthermore, this chapter considers the role of feminist movements in challenging and transforming power structures. It examines how feminist activism has influenced policy-making and societal values, promoting greater equity and inclusion. Through case studies and theoretical perspectives, we uncover the ways in which gender and power intersect to shape our social realities.

In conclusion, gender and power are deeply interconnected, with profound implications for individual and societal development. By understanding the dynamics of gender and power, we can better appreciate the potential for promoting gender equality and social justice.

15

Chapter 15: Future Trends in Power Structures

As we look to the future, it is essential to consider the emerging trends that will shape power structures in the coming decades. This chapter explores the key trends and challenges that will influence power dynamics, from technological advancements to demographic shifts and environmental changes.

We analyze the potential impact of emerging technologies, such as artificial intelligence, blockchain, and biotechnology, on power dynamics. The chapter addresses issues such as the ethical implications of these technologies, the potential for new forms of power and control, and the opportunities for promoting greater equity and inclusion.

Furthermore, this chapter considers the role of demographic and environmental changes in shaping future power structures. It examines how factors such as aging populations, urbanization, and climate change will influence power dynamics, creating new challenges and opportunities for governance and social justice.

In conclusion, future trends in power structures will shape the world in profound ways, with implications for individuals, communities, and institutions. By understanding these trends, we can better navigate the complexities of the future and promote more inclusive and sustainable forms of development.

Chapter 16: Strategies for Empowerment and Change

Empowerment and change are essential for promoting social justice and equity. This chapter explores the strategies and approaches that can be used to empower individuals and communities and drive transformative change.

We analyze the role of advocacy and activism in promoting social change, highlighting the diverse methods and tactics that can be used to challenge and transform power structures. The chapter addresses issues such as community organizing, policy advocacy, and the role of education and awareness-raising in promoting empowerment.

Furthermore, this chapter considers the role of collaboration and partnerships in driving change. It examines how different actors—from governments to civil society to the private sector—can work together to promote greater equity and inclusion. Through case studies and theoretical perspectives, we uncover the ways in which collective action can create lasting social change.

In conclusion, strategies for empowerment and change are crucial for promoting social justice and equity. By understanding these strategies, we can better appreciate the potential for individuals and communities to challenge and transform power structures.

17

Chapter 17: The Vision for a United Future

As we conclude our exploration of power, it is essential to consider the vision for a united future. This chapter explores the ways in which we can work towards a more inclusive, equitable, and sustainable world, where power is exercised in ways that promote the well-being of all.

We analyze the principles and values that underpin a vision for a united future, highlighting the importance of justice, equity, and solidarity. The chapter addresses issues such as the role of governance, the importance of inclusive decision-making, and the need for global cooperation and collaboration.

Furthermore, this chapter considers the role of individuals and communities in shaping the future. It examines how we can promote greater engagement and participation, empowering individuals and communities to take an active role in shaping their destinies. Through case studies and theoretical perspectives, we uncover the ways in which we can work together to create a more united and just world.

In conclusion, the vision for a united future is a powerful and inspiring goal that requires collective action and commitment. By understanding the principles and values that underpin this vision, we can better appreciate the potential for creating a more inclusive, equitable, and sustainable world.

18

Chapter 18: Power and Resilience

Resilience is a crucial aspect of power, enabling individuals, communities, and institutions to adapt and thrive in the face of challenges. This chapter explores the relationship between power and resilience, examining how resilience can be fostered and leveraged to promote social and economic well-being.

We analyze the role of resilience in shaping power dynamics, highlighting the ways in which resilient systems and structures can withstand and adapt to disruptions. The chapter addresses issues such as the importance of social and economic safety nets, the role of community support and solidarity, and the impact of resilience on individual and collective empowerment.

Furthermore, this chapter considers the strategies and approaches that can be used to promote resilience. It examines how different actors—from governments to civil society to the private sector—can work together to build more resilient systems and structures. Through case studies and theoretical perspectives, we uncover the ways in which resilience can be leveraged to create more inclusive and sustainable forms of power.

In conclusion, power and resilience are deeply interconnected, with profound implications for social and economic well-being. By understanding the dynamics of power and resilience, we can better appreciate the potential for fostering resilience and promoting social and economic justice.

19

Chapter 19: Power and Ethics

Ethics play a crucial role in shaping power dynamics, influencing the behavior and decisions of individuals and institutions. This chapter explores the relationship between power and ethics, examining the ways in which ethical considerations can guide the exercise of power.

We analyze the ethical challenges associated with power, highlighting issues such as corruption, abuse of power, and conflicts of interest. The chapter addresses the importance of ethical leadership and the role of values and principles in guiding decision-making.

Furthermore, this chapter considers the role of ethical frameworks and standards in promoting accountability and transparency. It examines how different sectors—from government to business to civil society—can adopt and implement ethical guidelines to promote responsible behavior. Through case studies and theoretical perspectives, we uncover the ways in which ethics can shape and transform power dynamics.

In conclusion, power and ethics are deeply interconnected, with profound implications for individual and societal well-being. By understanding the role of ethics in shaping power, we can better appreciate the potential for promoting accountability and social justice.

20

Chapter 20: Power and Innovation

Innovation is a powerful force that shapes the future of societies, driving economic growth and social progress. This chapter explores the relationship between power and innovation, examining how different actors—from governments to corporations to entrepreneurs—can leverage innovation to exercise and transform power.

We analyze the role of innovation in shaping power dynamics, highlighting the ways in which new technologies and business models can disrupt existing power structures. The chapter addresses issues such as the impact of innovation on economic competitiveness, the role of intellectual property, and the importance of fostering a culture of innovation.

Furthermore, this chapter considers the challenges and opportunities associated with innovation. It examines how innovation can promote greater equity and inclusion, as well as the potential risks and unintended consequences of technological advancements. Through case studies and theoretical perspectives, we uncover the ways in which innovation can both empower and challenge different actors.

In conclusion, power and innovation are deeply interconnected, with profound implications for economic and social development. By understanding the dynamics of innovation and its impact on power, we can better navigate the complexities of the future and promote more inclusive and sustainable forms of progress.

21

Chapter 21: Power and Conflict Resolution

onflict is an inevitable aspect of human interaction, with power dynamics playing a crucial role in shaping the causes and outcomes of conflicts. This chapter explores the relationship between power and conflict resolution, examining the ways in which power influences the processes and outcomes of resolving conflicts.

We analyze the role of power in shaping conflict dynamics, highlighting the ways in which power imbalances can exacerbate or mitigate conflicts. The chapter addresses issues such as the role of mediation and negotiation, the importance of dialogue and communication, and the impact of power on peacebuilding efforts.

Furthermore, this chapter considers the strategies and approaches that can be used to promote conflict resolution. It examines how different actors—from governments to civil society to international organizations—can work together to address conflicts and promote sustainable peace. Through case studies and theoretical perspectives, we uncover the ways in which power can be leveraged to resolve conflicts and promote social cohesion.

In conclusion, power and conflict resolution are deeply interconnected, with profound implications for social and political stability. By understanding the dynamics of power and conflict, we can better appreciate the potential for promoting peace and resolving conflicts in ways that promote justice and equity.

Book Description:

In "The Nexus of Power: Uniting Political Theory, Social Dynamics, and Corporate Vision," readers embark on a compelling journey through the intricate realms of power. This thought-provoking book delves into the multifaceted nature of power, exploring its manifestations in political ideologies, social dynamics, and corporate governance.

The book opens with a solid foundation, tracing the historical evolution of power and its influence on societies. It examines key political ideologies and their impact on power structures, offering valuable insights into the workings of political institutions and governance. The role of social movements in challenging and transforming power is also explored, highlighting the potential for collective action to drive social change.

As readers navigate through the chapters, they will uncover the profound impact of corporate power on modern capitalism and its implications for economies and societies. The book delves into the interplay of politics and economics, analyzing the complexities of global power dynamics and the influence of media and public opinion.

The digital age, with its transformative technologies, is examined for its impact on power distribution, while environmental policy and health are explored as critical areas where power dynamics play out. The book also addresses the role of education, cultural power, and workplace dynamics in shaping power structures, emphasizing the importance of equity and inclusion.

Towards the end, the book looks to the future, considering emerging trends and challenges that will shape power structures in the coming decades. It offers strategies for empowerment and change, promoting social justice and equity, and envisions a united future where power is exercised in ways that promote the well-being of all.

"The Nexus of Power" is a must-read for anyone interested in understanding the complexities of power and its implications for contemporary society. It provides a comprehensive analysis of power dynamics, offering valuable insights and practical strategies for promoting more inclusive and sustainable forms of development.